Looking After Rock Pools

Written by Kerrie Shanahan

Flying Start
to Literacy®

T0342932

We went on a school excursion to the Marine Discovery Centre. At the Centre we met Karly Chan, who is a marine biologist.

Karly knows a lot about sea animals and plants. We asked Karly lots of questions to find out about what she does.

Q Why do you teach people about rock pools?

A I teach people about the ocean and the shore and how to look after them.

Some of the time I teach in a special classroom where people can see and touch marine animals.

I take people snorkelling so they can see animals in the sea. I also take people for walks on the beach where we explore rock pools.

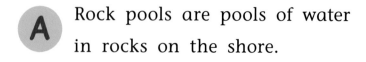 Q What are rock pools?

A Rock pools are pools of water in rocks on the shore.

Rocks on the shore are covered in water when the tide comes in. When the tide goes out, some water is left behind in the pool.

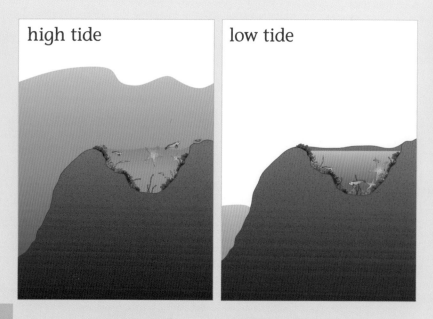

high tide

low tide

The tide is important to rock pools.
The tide comes in and out every day.
When the tide comes in, it brings in
clean sea water.

This water also brings lots of tiny animals called plankton into the rock pools.
Many animals in rock pools eat plankton.

plankton

Q Why are rock pools interesting?

A Looking in rock pools is a great way for people to learn about sea life and how animals and plants live together. People can see a huge range of animals in one small place.

Q Which animals live in rock pools?

A Rock pools are home to many animals. Rock pools help to protect these animals from strong tides and powerful waves. Without rock pools these animals could not survive on the rocky shore.

These are some of the animals that live
in rock pools.

octopus

shrimp

crab

anemone

sea snail

sea star

13

Q What grows in rock pools?

A Seaweed grows in rock pools. There are different types of seaweeds.

Animals in rock pools use the seaweed in different ways. Some animals eat seaweed, some use it for shelter and some use it to hide from other animals that might eat them.

Q How do we stay safe when exploring rock pools?

A Always check the weather conditions before exploring rock pools. In wet, stormy weather the waves can be dangerous.

You have to be careful not to stand too close to where the waves are breaking because the waves can wash you into the sea. Rock pools can be wet and slippery so you must walk carefully.

Never pick up an animal that you don't recognise because some animals in rock pools can be dangerous.

Q What happens when there is rubbish in rock pools?

A When rubbish is dropped on the beach or into the sea, it can be washed into rock pools.

When there is rubbish in a rock pool and the water is dirty, the animals that live there can become sick and die.

Q What happens if we take things from rock pools?

A Plants and animals that are taken out of rock pools often die because they cannot survive away from the rock pool.

If one type of plant or animal disappears from the rock pool, this can affect other plants and animals.

For example, if too many shrimp or crabs are taken away from the rock pool it could become dirty. Shrimp and crabs help to keep the rock pool clean.

Hermit crabs live in shells in rock pools. If you take away the shells, then the hermit crabs have nowhere to live.

Q What can we do to look after rock pools?

A Everyone can help to look after rock pools.

When you visit the beach, make sure you do these things:

- Take your rubbish with you when you leave. Rubbish at the beach can end up in rock pools.

- Always read the signs at the beach and do as they say.

- Leave everything in a rock pool as you found it.

DOGS
OHIBITED

23

Q What is your most important message about rock pools?

A If we look after rock pools, the animals that live there will have a healthy home and we can continue to enjoy seeing them.